That's Extreme!

Jo Chambers

Contents

Safe or crazy?	2
Snowboarding	4
Kayaking	6
Skydiving	8
Parachuting	10
Street luging	12
Climbing	14
Stunts on bikes	16
Moto X racing	18
Whitewater rafting	20
Skating and skateboarding	22
Sum up	24

OXFORD
UNIVERSITY PRESS

Safe or crazy?

Name the sports in the photos. Which are played at your school? Think of 3 more.

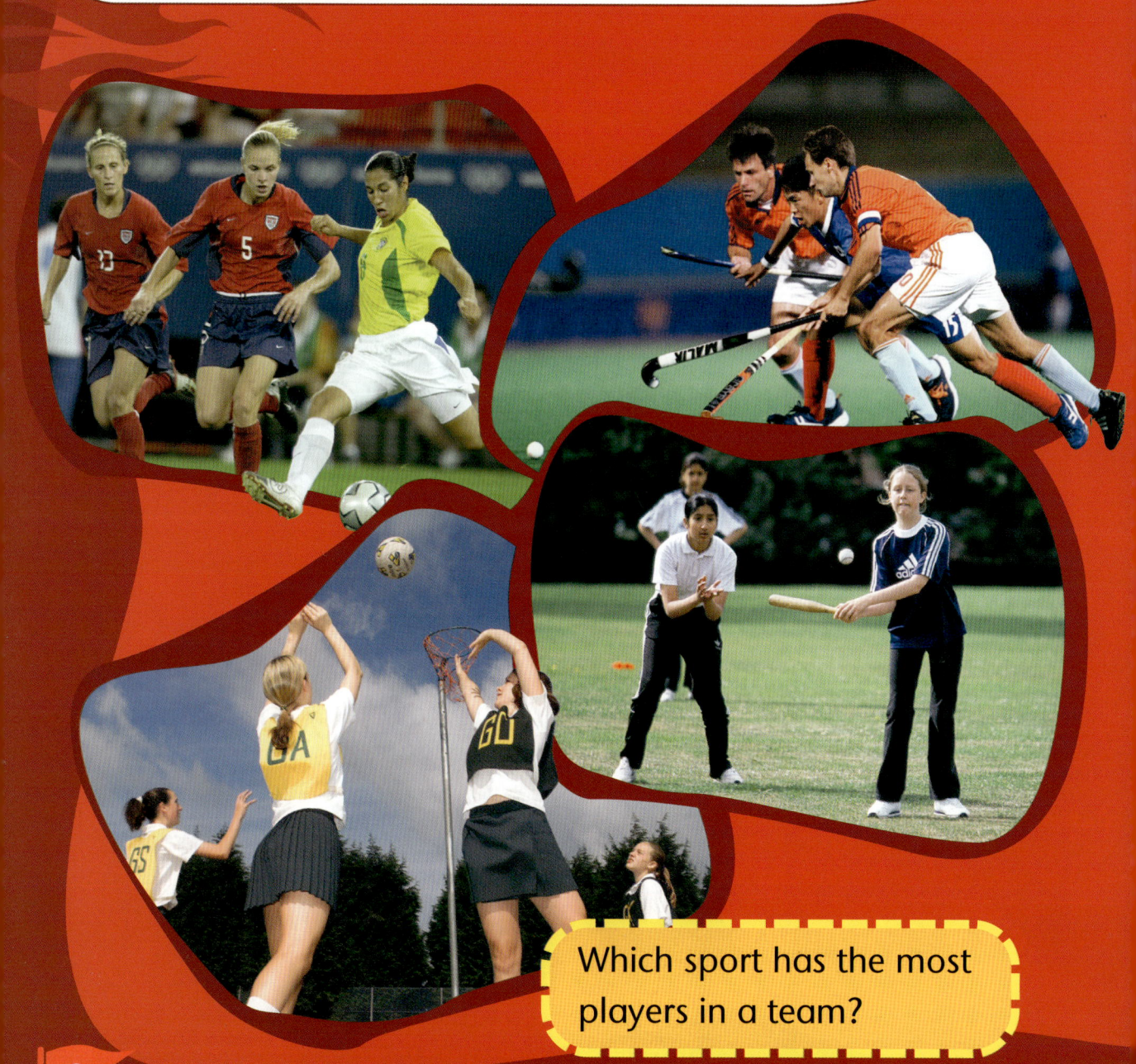

Which sport has the most players in a team?

KEY WORDS

- more
- describe
- how many?
- shape

Some people find those sports boring. They want more of a challenge.

This is bungee jumping – it's an EXTREME SPORT!

Describe the photo to a friend. How many shape words can you use?

TOOLS

square   rectangle   triangle   pentagon   circle

3

Snowboarding

Snowboarding is like surfing on snow. Freestyle boarding includes tricks like spins and jumps.

FACT! The average sized board is about 150 cm long and 25 cm wide.

Guess the number of skis and ski poles in this photo. Then count them.

Point to shapes in the picture with 4 corners.

This snowboarder is 'riding the pipe'. The 'pipe' is made of snow and curves from the ground upwards creating a slope. Name some shapes with curved faces.

KEY WORDS

- corner
- curved face
- circle
- rectangle

What is this snowboarder doing? Find circles and rectangles in the picture. Name other shapes you can see.

TOOLS

circle rectangle triangle cylinder cone

5

Kayaking

- A kayak is a small strong boat used in fast flowing water.

- The paddle is long, narrow and symmetrical.

- This kayaker is going through heavy rapids. Describe the equipment he's using.

There are different types of kayak. Some are for one person, others for two people. Longer kayaks are easier to keep in a straight line. Shorter kayaks can turn round bends more easily.

KEY WORDS
- straight
- turn
- fold
- size

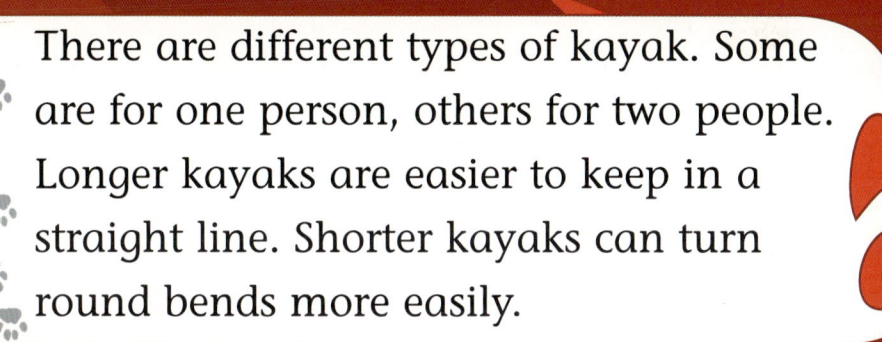

folding kayak

rigid kayaks

inflatable kayak

Which type of kayak would be the lightest? Explain your thinking.

Choose a kayak to hire for a short trip for 2 people down fast rapids. Think about size, length and material.

TOOLS

single – double   long – short   light – heavy

Skydiving

Skydivers jump from planes high in the air. They wait before opening their parachutes and fall very fast.

Freefall gymnastics – skydivers do a set routine of loops and turns as quickly as possible.

parachute

Skysurfing – skydivers on surfboards do loops, barrel rolls, helicopter spins, avalanches and nose-curves. Draw the shapes you think these moves make.

surfboard

FACT! 350 skydivers linked together in the sky to save lives in 2004.

KEY WORDS

- circular
- turn
- corner
- pentagon

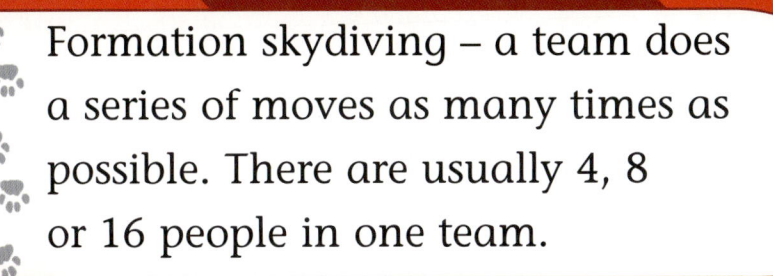

Formation skydiving – a team does a series of moves as many times as possible. There are usually 4, 8 or 16 people in one team.

In this photo the skydivers have joined hands making a circular shape. What shapes can be made by joining 4 corners?

formation

TOOLS

4 Corners

Is it possible to make a pentagon? Explain your thinking.

Parachuting

Parachutes come in different shapes and sizes. Most of them are circular or rectangular.

Make a list of other circular and rectangular things.

5cm

FACT! Skydivers jump from 3 thousand feet in the air and try to land on a circular spot only 5 cm across. This is called accuracy landing.

KEY WORDS

- rectangular
- circular
- patterns
- symmetrical

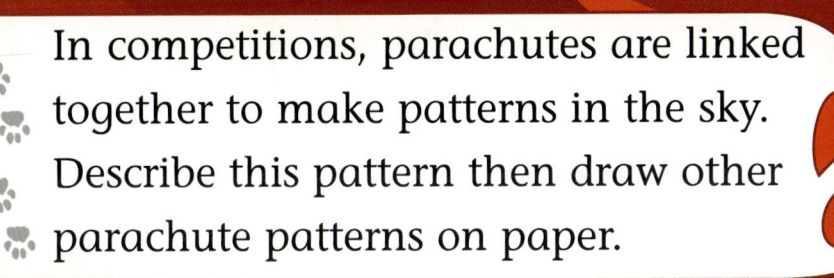

In competitions, parachutes are linked together to make patterns in the sky. Describe this pattern then draw other parachute patterns on paper.

Make symmetrical patterns using 9 parachutes.

These 6 army paratroopers are landing. What might houses and fields look like from above?

TOOLS

circular    rectangular    triangular

Street luging

- Street luging is a dangerous high-speed sport. The riders lie flat on a luge and race down steep roads. They can reach speeds of 130 km per hour.

FACT! The luge is like a long skateboard made from aluminium.

- Look at the lines in the road. What do you notice?

- Lugers change direction by leaning from side to side. Which direction are these lugers moving in? Which luger is in front?

luge

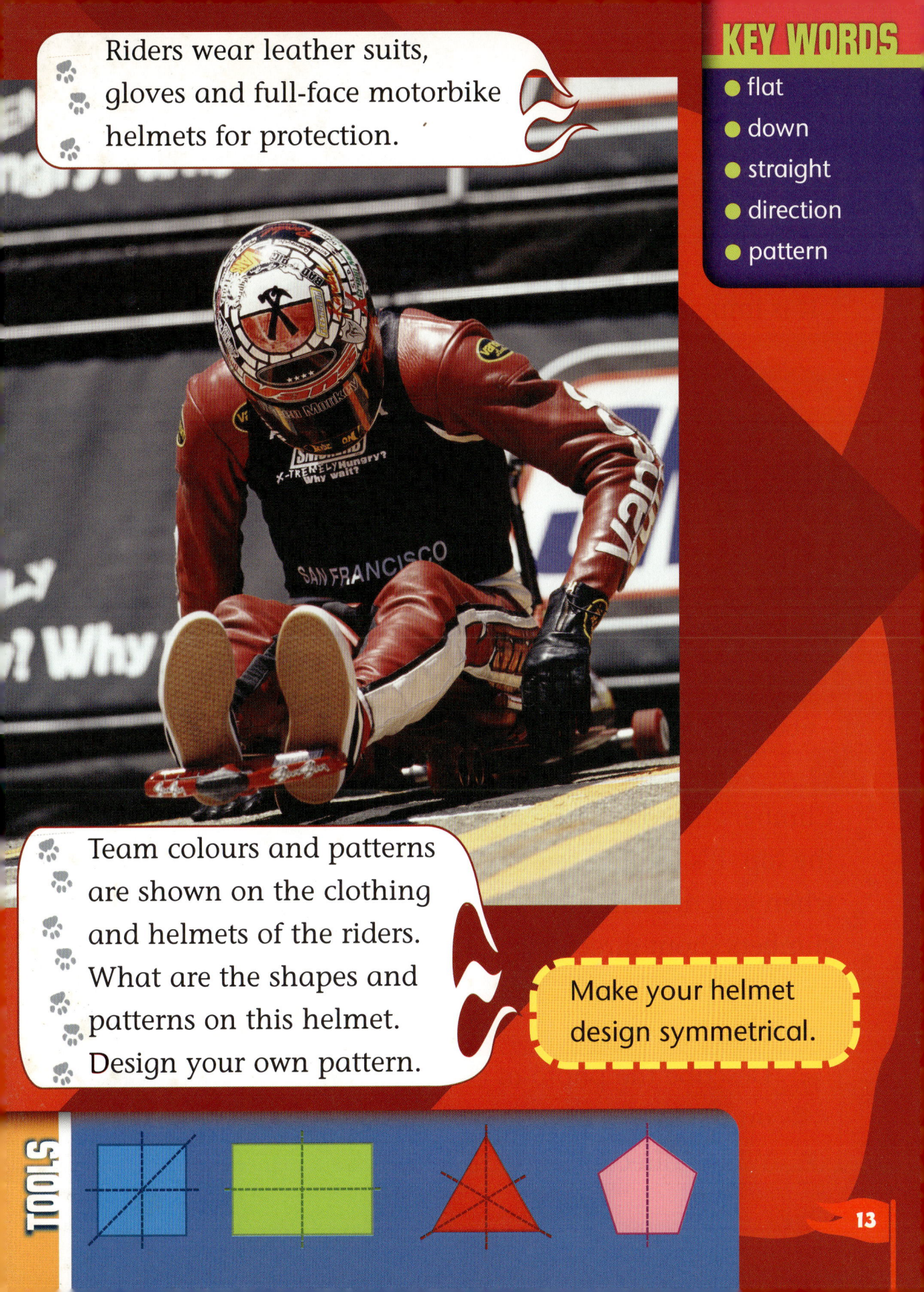

Riders wear leather suits, gloves and full-face motorbike helmets for protection.

KEY WORDS
- flat
- down
- straight
- direction
- pattern

Team colours and patterns are shown on the clothing and helmets of the riders. What are the shapes and patterns on this helmet. Design your own pattern.

Make your helmet design symmetrical.

TOOLS

13

Climbing

- There are different types of climbing.
- It is important to find good 'holds'.

traditional rock climbing

indoor wall climbing

- Climbers try to find the best way to the top. It's hard to see where to go when you are climbing. Other climbers shout directions to them.

- Describe the photo of climbers on the indoor climbing wall.
- Which directions can they go?

The rocks in this photo look like they are carefully balancing on each other. Which 3D shapes can be stacked on top of each other like this? Record your ideas as sketches.

KEY WORDS
- left
- right
- directions
- cone
- pyramid

Could a cone or pyramid be halfway up the stack? Explain your answer.

FACT! If a climber manages the whole route first time it is called an 'on-sight flash'.

TOOLS

cone   pyramid   cuboid   cube   sphere   cylinder

Stunts on bikes

Mountain bikers race each other over a natural course. They have to jump over obstacles.

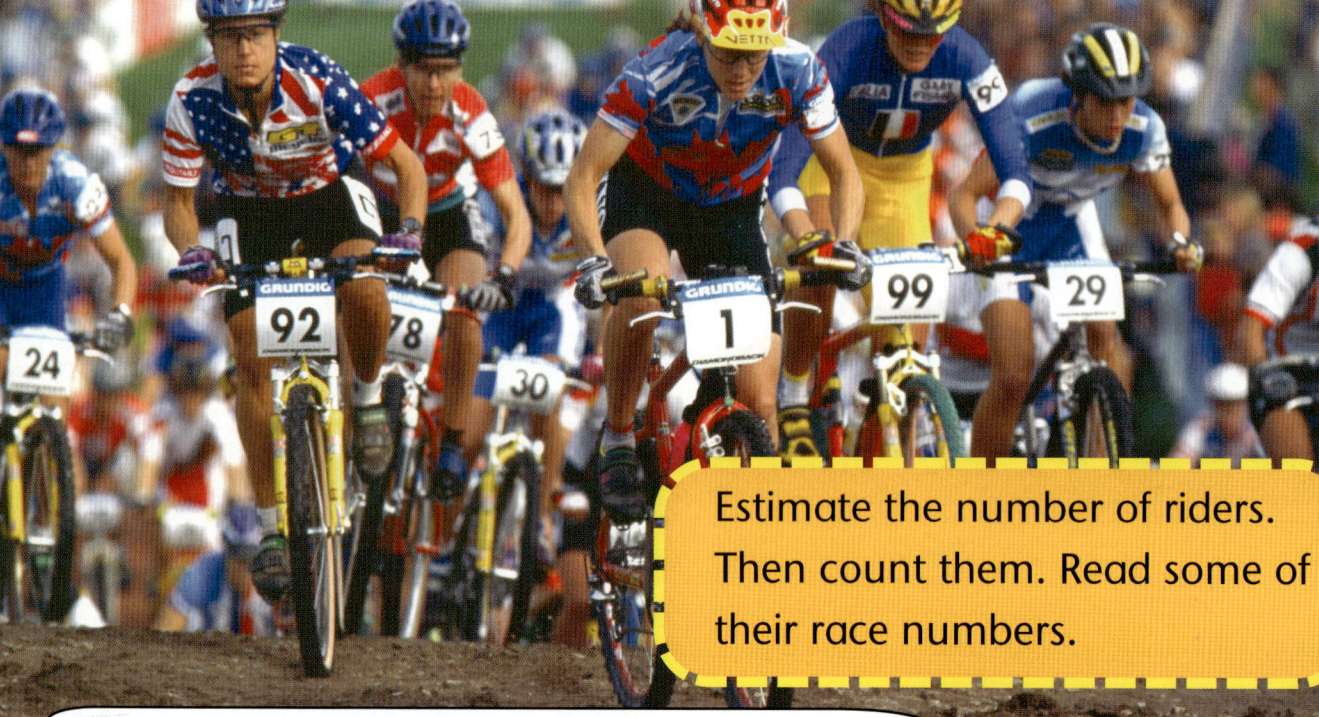

Estimate the number of riders. Then count them. Read some of their race numbers.

How to jump over a fallen tree trunk.

1 Sit down and pedal fast.

2 Stand and pull the handlebars up to lift the front wheel over the tree.

3 Lean forward to help the back wheel over the tree.

KEY WORDS
- corner
- position
- star
- forward

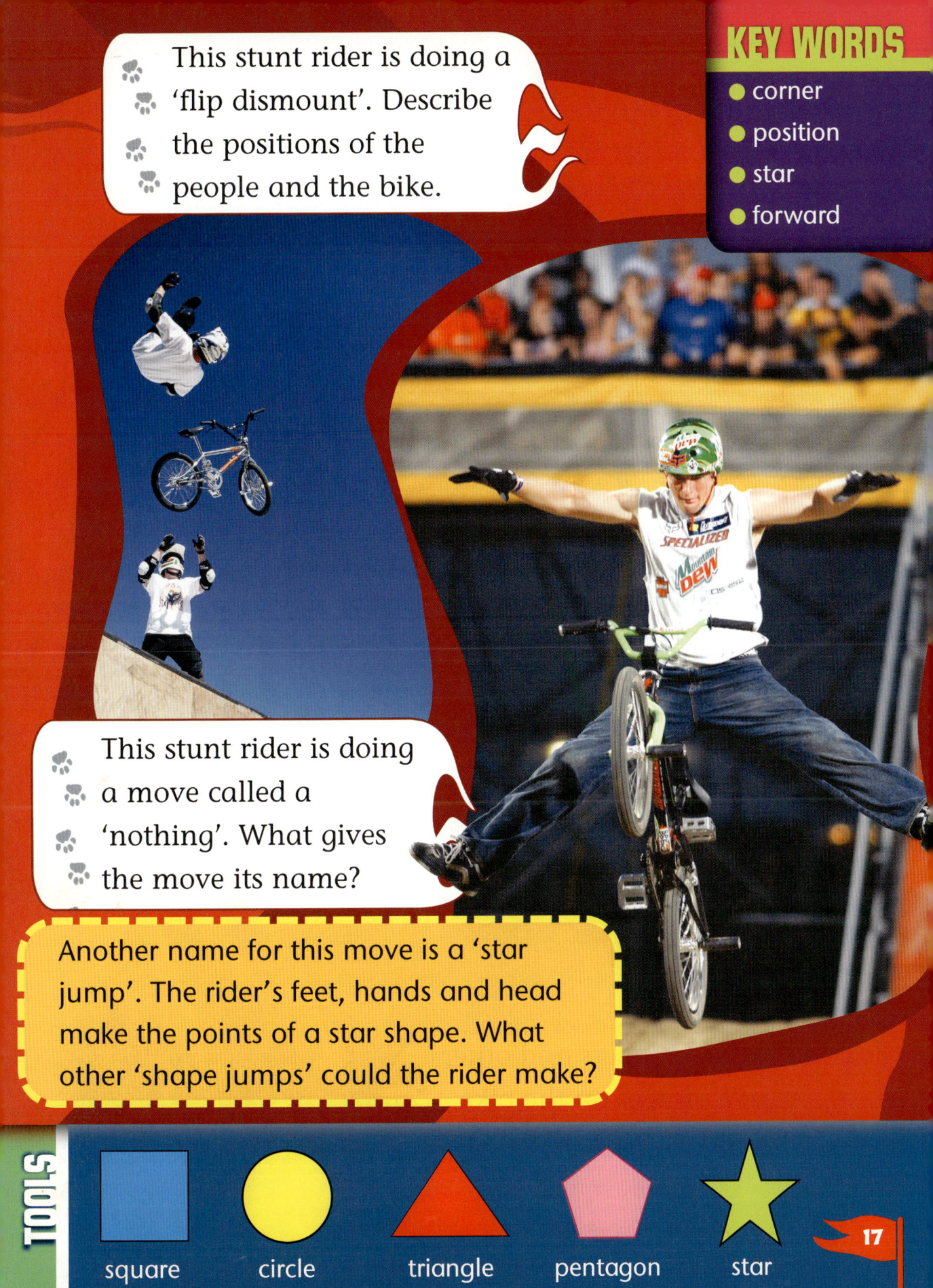

This stunt rider is doing a 'flip dismount'. Describe the positions of the people and the bike.

This stunt rider is doing a move called a 'nothing'. What gives the move its name?

Another name for this move is a 'star jump'. The rider's feet, hands and head make the points of a star shape. What other 'shape jumps' could the rider make?

TOOLS

square   circle   triangle   pentagon   star

17

Moto X racing

In moto X ('moto-cross') riders race each other cross-country. Which bike is in the lead? How many are following behind?

Look for cylinders and other circular shapes on the bike.

These riders are doing freestyle stunts. Each one has twisted, turned or jumped to get into position.

Compare the different stunt positions. Describe what they might do next, try to use some of these words: over, under, below, in front, behind, middle.

KEY WORDS
- cylinder
- circular
- turn
- over
- under

Think up some more stunt positions for the riders.

TOOLS

turn left turn right

Whitewater rafting

🐾 Whitewater rafting is when teams of people paddle through water rapids and down huge river drops.

hard hat

oar

white water

inflatable dinghy

life jackets

🐾 Count the people inside this raft. Why do you think they are sitting round the outside of it?

Draw a picture to show what the dinghy looks like from above.

KEY WORDS

- edge
- inside
- triangular
- left
- right

This raft is going down some rapids. How many people do you think will fall out?

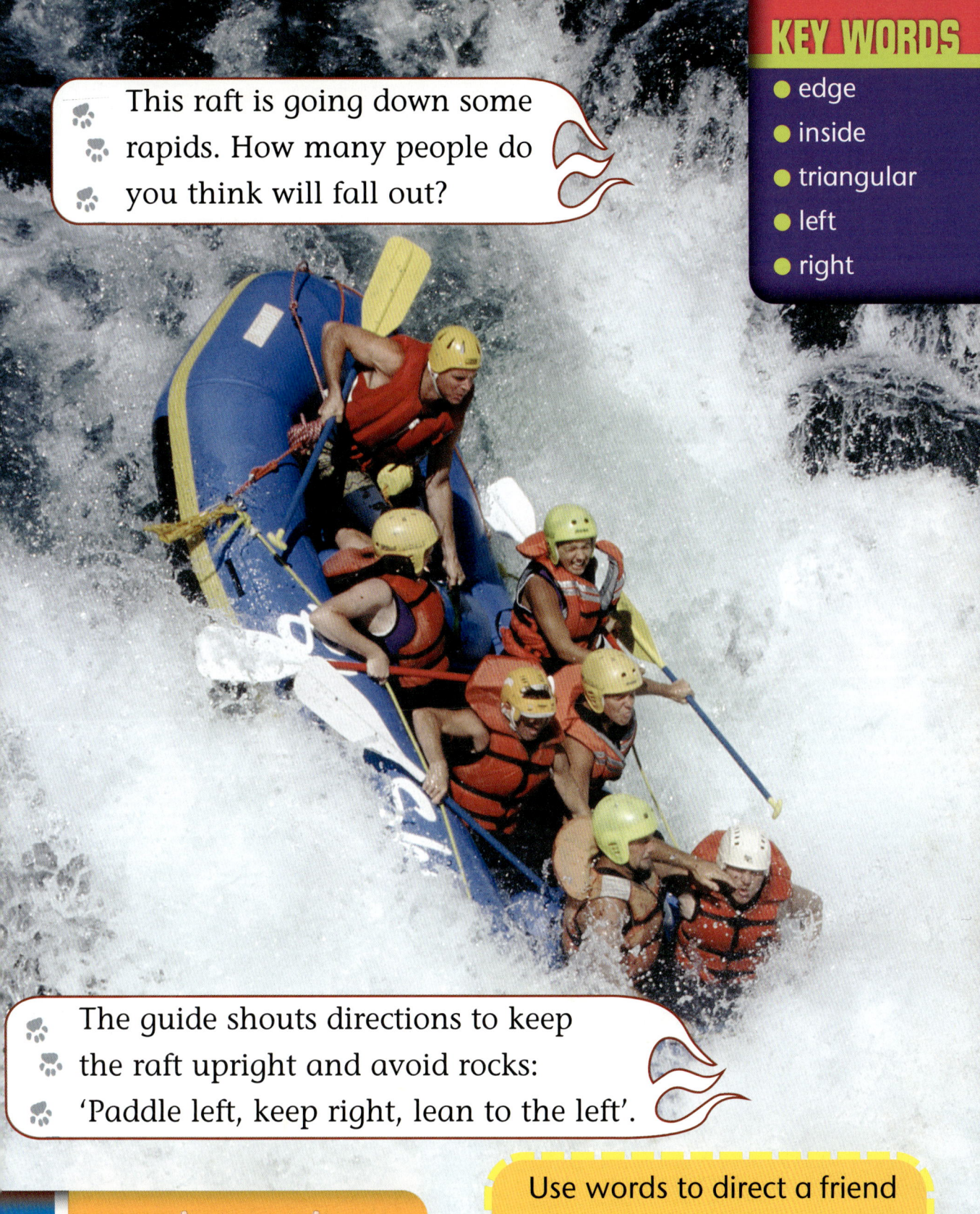

The guide shouts directions to keep the raft upright and avoid rocks: 'Paddle left, keep right, lean to the left'.

Use words to direct a friend through an obstacle course.

TOOLS

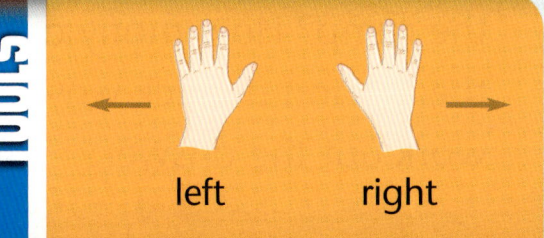

left   right

Skating and skateboarding

- In-line skaters race to complete a circuit.
- They also do tricks, spins and jumps.

- Skate boots have 4 wheels in a line. Describe the boot wheels this skater is using.

The fastest speed for skating is over 100 km per hour. FACT!

What tile shapes are on the ramp? How many are there? Find a quick way to work out the answer.

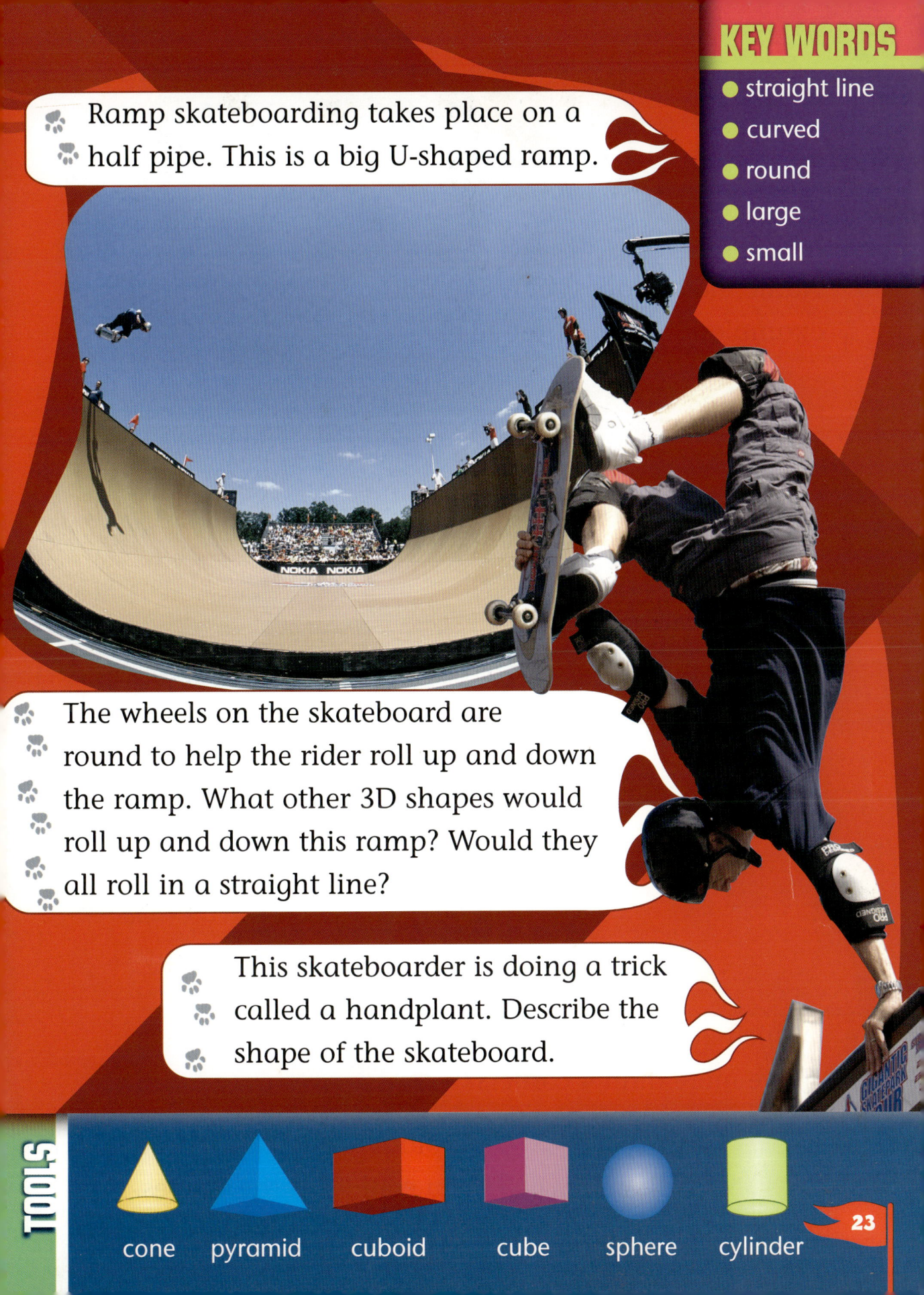

KEY WORDS

- straight line
- curved
- round
- large
- small

Ramp skateboarding takes place on a half pipe. This is a big U-shaped ramp.

The wheels on the skateboard are round to help the rider roll up and down the ramp. What other 3D shapes would roll up and down this ramp? Would they all roll in a straight line?

This skateboarder is doing a trick called a handplant. Describe the shape of the skateboard.

TOOLS

cone   pyramid   cuboid   cube   sphere   cylinder

Sum up

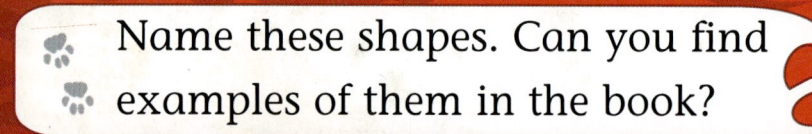

🐾 Name these shapes. Can you find examples of them in the book?

🐾 Which 2D shapes above have more than 4 corners?

🐾 Explain some different ways you could sort the shapes.